FIDDLE
FADDLE
FUDDLE

Sense and Nonsense

by

DAN PRINTUP

THE BLUE AND GRAY BOOK SHOP
Publishers
3537 Walker at Highland Avenue
Memphis, Tennessee

Manufactured in the U.S.A.
McCowat-Mercer Press, Inc.
Jackson, Tenn.

To Enoch and Ara Mitchell for their
kindness in laughing at my nonsense
and their boldness in backing it.

Ambition is a greedy jade
Who'll make a drudge of you,
Unless you have the happy gift
Of being foolish too.

CONTENTS

NONSENSE

CONTENTS

NONSENSE

CONTENTS

SENSE

FIDDLE, FADDLE, FUDDLE

I'll never be rich, and that's no joke.
I'll always be flat or almost broke,
Because the things I ought to do
Are about as dull as a worn out shoe.
    So—I fiddle.

My lights are battered and my film tank leaks,
The tripod slips and the printer creaks,
But there's some music I want to hear
And the day is so gloomy and dark and drear—
    Oh, faddle!

The windows are stained 'till I can't see out
And the rains have washed the drive about.
There are millions of leaves that I should rake,
But there's a table I want to make.
    So—I fuddle.

The telephone jangles and customers yell,
But I just say, "Oh, hang that bell!
Don't they know there's a toy I want to make,
And maybe a pie or two to bake?"
    And—I fiddle.

So now it's almost ten o'clock
And I should go down and get a stock
Of photo supplies and frames and such,
But I can't get interested very much.
    Aw—faddle!

Black Boy needs a bath again
And the floor's all muddy where I let him in.
I should get busy and clean them both,
But somehow I just sit and loaf.
    And fuddle.

It seems remote, but it must be true,
Some day I'll find that I'm all through,
And unless I change my ways a heap
It's a darn slim harvest I will reap.
    Because I fiddle, faddle, fuddle.

CHRISMUS GIF'

Chrismus gif', Miss Molly!
I know dere's boun' to be
A present for ol' Mandy
On dat great big Chrismus tree.

Lawd, ain't dat a beauty!
Hit sho a pretty sight.
Dem little lights a-shinin'
An' dat star mos' outer sight!

Ain't dem little chillun
Havin' deysef a time!
Look at all de toys dey got
An' little books dat rhyme.

I done had my brekfus,
But sho would be real nice
Ef I could have some coffee
'Fore traipsin' through dat ice.

Thank you mam! Miss Molly!
Lordy, ain't dat fine?
New dress sho look fancy
'Side dese ol' rags uv mine.

It always make me happy,
Jus' give my soul a lif',
To come up to de big house
An' ketch you "Chrismus gif'!"

NO GOOD GAL

Sam ask me where I git dat gal
Wid de painted face an' lips,
Big gold tooth an' de arched eyebrows,
An' dem real free-swingin' hips.

She say she want to make a crop
On dat little farm I got.
Sam say, "Dat's yo' bizness,
But she look like a sorry lot."

"You go down dere an' stir aroun'
An' work like de very dickens,
But I give you odds dat fancy wench
Won't even feed de chickens."

Sam was right, an' she's a mess
An' she won't milk or plow.
Hit was fun for a little while,
But I'se in a big mess now.

De sheriff is a frien' of mine.
If he come nosin' 'round,
I bet dat no good fancy gal
Gonna high tail out for town.

Guess I'll talk to de sheriff
Soon as dese 'lasses thicken,
'Cause I ain't gonna feed no gal
Dat won't even feed de chickens!

NOW HEAR DIS

The "Reverend" Williams cleared his throat,
For the first time faced his flock.
He opened up his Bible
And glanced up at the clock.

" 'Fore I begins my ministry,
I wants to clear some things —
I wants no buttons in de plate,
An' I wants you all to sing."

"Now I cain't please each livin' soul,
So I ain't a-gonna try —
I know some heads for heaven
An' some is gonna fry."

"Some folks is bounden to be mean,
But some is really saints,
An' so some says, 'Dey ain't no hell,'
An de res', 'De hell dey ain't!' "

"I'se gonna pray an' work real hard
To save you folks from sin,
An' when you 'grees wid what I say,
Bear down wid a big AMEN!"

"So now you understan's me
An' de hour is gittin' late.
Les sing hymn ninety-seben —
Uh, Deacon Jones, please pass de plate."

RATS

Amos lived on my uncle's farm,
And he was a real good hand.
But Amos always did aspire
To being a learned man.

When he had a letter to be "writ"
He'd ease into the store
And peck on that old Oliver
For an hour — maybe more.

One day he struggled manfully
With a letter to some gal.
Could be it was Carrie,
Or Susie — maybe Sal.

Amos scratched his kinky head
And wrinkled his ebony brow,
Then tapped a few typewriter keys —
He could easier run a plow.

Then, turning to Uncle Bill, he asked,
"Boss, how does you spell rat?"
"R-a-t," Uncle Bill replied,
"It's just as easy as that."

Amos thought a minute,
Then this he did allow —
"I don' mean rat like mouse rat,
I mean rat like *rat now!*"

CRACKLIN BREAD

Some folks say it's a real hard life,
A-livin' on a farm,
An' so it is, 'less you got good food
An' a house dat's good an' warm.
But dere's some things 'bout country life
Dat elsewheres you cain't find
An' mention of ernough to eat
Brings cracklin' bread to mind.

Cracklin' bread! Lordy me,
It pictures in my mind
Crops all in, an' de wood stacked up
An' den hog killin' time!
Now you jus' let me talk a spell,
An' I'll tell you how its done,
How to have de fines' vittles
Under heaven's shinin' sun!

You wait for a day dat's nice an' crisp,
Wid frost sparklin' all aroun',
Dat's de bes' time to fix yo' meat,
'Cause it keep real good an' soun'.
You trims de hams an' bacon,
An' de ribs an' backbone too.
Den you puts de fat in a big black pot
An' sets it on to stew.

Now de lard it cook out from de fat
An' leave little golden bits,
An' dey's de worl's bes' eatin'

As sure as here I sits!
Dey's what de folks calls cracklin's,
An' dey so sweet an' brown
You jus' cain't hardly stan' it
'Till supper time come roun'.

Now git yo'sef some collard greens
Dat de fros' done made real sweet,
An' den spare ribs an' dumplin's.
Man! Dat's good to eat!
Den maybe some mashed up 'taters,
An' coffee good an' black,
An' blackberry jam an' butter,
Den dere's one mo' thing you lack.

Bread—not jus' any bread,
Cracklin' bread's de thing.
Dat's de stuff to happy yo' mouf
An' make yo' stummick sing.
Made wid fresh groun' corn meal,
Yaller, or even white,
De cracklin's mixed in de batter,
An' you got some bread dat's right!

I know dis ain't no fancy food,
But it sho' stick to yo' rib,
So go ahead an' smack yo' lips
An' spill it on yo bib.
It starts my mouf a-waterin',
An' I'd jus' as soon be dead
As have to live in a stuffy town
Eatin' cake stead of cracklin' bread.

PROCEDURE

How come I bus' dat mule in de face
Wid dis here stick er wood,
After tellin' you to treat him kind
An' den he work real good?

Well, I'm gonna tell you how it is,
One thing I forgot to mention.
Before dat mule pay you any mind,
You firs' got to get his attention.

HE DON'T MIND

Uncle Mose is a real old man,
Wid a snow white, kinky head,
But he says, "I don't mind gittin' old.
When you stops gittin' old, you dead!"

FIRED AGAIN

How come you settin' on dem steps
A-fryin' in de sun?
You better git back in dat house
An' git yo' cleanin' done!

I cain't go back inside de house.
Miss Molly riled agin.
She got a misery in her back,
An', gal, she mean as sin!

She fire me little while ago,
Say, "Jus' git out my sight!"
"Yassum," I say, an' come out here
'Till she gits a mite mo' right.

I cain't go off cause won't be long
'Fore she be lookin' for me,
An' if I ain't a-hangin' 'round
She be mad as she can be.

Dat's why Miss Molly'n me is frien's,
Jus' like we always been,
'Cause I know when she fire me
She soon hire me back agin.

JOHNSON GRASS

I had a patch
Of Johnson grass
In a bottom land corn field.
The stuff when scratched
As plows went past,
Spread with vicious zeal.

I asked old Mose
Could he tell me
A way to beat the mess.
He scratched his nose,
Said, "Lemme see —"
And hunkered down to rest.

Then with a gold-toothed,
Gate-wide grin,
He said, you can believe it,
"De onlies' way, an' it's de truf,
Is move agin an' leave it."

'POSSUM

Chicken squawk,
Grab my gun,
To de hen house
Fast I run.
'Possum hidin',
See him dere,
Easy shot wid
Room to spare.

'Possum brownin'
In de stove
Wid dem 'taters
Dat I love.
Should have quit,
Took his winnin's,
Stuck to eatin'
Fros' sweet 'simmons.

HELP!

Rufus caught a wildcat,
Which was a grievous error.
The critter clawed and slashed him,
And Rufus shrieked with terror.

Mose heard all the rumpus,
And came up on the double.
"Want me to help you hold him, boy?
You look like you got trouble!"

"Lordy, naw!" Squalled Rufus.
"Come here you stupid goose!
Grab a-holt of this here thing
An' help me turn him loose!"

JUS' RIGHT

Mr. Benny gimme a drink of likker,
An' I downed it quick as yo' eye can flicker.
Mr. Benny laughed wid all his might.
I say, "Mr. Benny, now dat's jus' right.
If it been any better you'd of drinked it first,
An' I couldn't drink it do it be any worse!"

HARD LUCK JOE

When I gets down an' sad an' blue,
An' feel like life is jus' all through,
Who says to me, "Man, I sure love you."?
Who says dat? - - - Nobody.

When I rolls twelves an' threes an' twos
'Till every cryin' dime I lose,
Who hands me a buck or two to use?
Who does dat? - - - Nobody.

When my pants is ragged an' my hide shine through,
An' my shoes done frayed an' split out, too,
Who says, "Here, dis suit an' shoes jus' fit you."?
Who says dat? - - - Nobody.

When I ain't had a decent meal,
An' I gotta eat if I hafter steal,
Who says to me, "Eat dis steak. Go on, it's real."?
Who says dat? - - - Nobody.

I've stomped aroun' dis worl' a lot,
An' it looks like trouble's all I got.
Tomorrow seem like it be jus' de same.
I try an' try, an' work an' sweat
An' I ain't got a damn thing yet;
They's jus' no way to win in dis here game.

So now I'se tired an' low in mind.
Whatever happen, I'se still behind.
Dere ain't no happy place dat I can go.
I'se give up hope dat things will change,
An' I'se jus' turned out on de range.
My name? I'se known as Hard Luck Joe.

I AIN'T GOIN' TO FRET!

Since I am always worryin'
About some thing or other,
I know this time a year ago
I had some great big bother,
But for the very life of me
I can't think what it was.
I don't know how it turned out
Or even what the cause.

An' so this current problem
That looks so tough to me,
Will fade like all the others,
An' even leave me free
To start another brand new crop
Of wrinkles in my brow,
An' I'll be darned if I will fret
An' worry 'bout it now!

NO SPOOKS

Pearly was a character.
His full name? Pearly Gates.
Though being teased about his name
Is one thing Pearly hates.
We hired him as a janitor
To clean around the place.
Though he did a fair to middling job,
No effort did he waste.

He was very careful with his broom,
And never wore one out,
But he said it wasn't 'cause he shirked—
They made the brooms too stout!
He did a messy cleaning job
But still we kept him 'round
'Cause Pearly was a part-time sage,
His thoughts sometimes profound.

He asked me what I thought of "hants."
I said, "There is no such."
He said, "I'se heard a lot of tales,
But I don't b'lieve 'em much.
Jus' step here to de door with me.
I'll show you what I mean.
See! Ev'ywhere a man can look,
Dey's a church house to be seen."

"You see dem big white columns?
Well, dat's de Baptis' Church.
De 'Piscopalians is down dere
Where all dem pigeons perch.
De Cat'olics goes over dere,
Where you see dat big gold cross.
De Methodis' is got dey church
Nex' do' to ol' man Ross.

"Den down de road's dat happy church.
Dey sho sings up a storm.
Dey clap and shout and get het up
Like a fo' bell fire alarm.
Dey's churches ev'y way you look
An' dey all is workin' hard
To keep de folks from sinful ways
An' bring 'em to de Lawd.

"Now if de devil git a man
He sho do have to work,
'Cause all dese folks is 'gin him
An' he cain't sit back an' shirk.
So when he git a sinful soul,
As sho as black is black,
He's gonna keep him down below
An' he never can come back!

"What heaven's like I jus' don't know,
But dis ol' world is rough.
Dey say up dere de streets is gold
An' de livin' ain't so tough.
You wears white robes an' halos
An' great, big, silky wings,
An' no ones got no troubles,
An' ev'ybody sings!

"Now you know well as I do
If a man can git in dere,
He ain't gonna have no intres'
In comin' back down here.
So ain't no spooks to worry 'bout
'Cause return de good folks ain't,
An' dem dat mean ol' devil got,
Come back dey sho'ly cain't."

EASY DOES IT

John was an ageing colored man
Who was working in my yard.
The task that day was a heavy one,
And the sun beat hot and hard.
His scrawny, stringy, corded arms
Looked too frail for the job,
And it seemed as though the blazing sun
His strength must surely rob.

He worked along at steady pace
And never seemed to stop
Except a moment now and then
His deep-lined face to mop.
Sweat had dampened all his clothes
And trickled off his chin.
I said, "Why don't you rest a bit,
Then start in fresh again?"

He leaned upon the shovel,
His head cocked to one side,
As he thought the matter over,
And then at last replied,
As he looked at me with a funny grin
And his wrinkled brow perspired,
"He may die hongry, an' he may die cold,
But John will not die tired."

PLEASE, LAWD!

De Good Book say dat I should be
My troubled brother's keeper,
Dat I should comfort dem in pain
An' aid de saddened weeper.
Dat I should help dem in distress,
De heartsick try to find.
I think dis sounds real good, Oh Lawd,
But who'll help me wid mine?

De storms of life has battered me
Until I'se jus' a wreck.
Dere's not much sunshine in dis world,
Sometimes not a speck!
My bag of burdens weighs me down
Until I slip and reel.
How can I take on any mo'
An' stay on even keel?

Dere's jus' one answer dat I see
If I'se to help some other.
Someone else must look aroun'
An' see dat I'se *his* brother —
But I don' look for nuthin'
As I stumble down de road,
So please, Lawd, cain't you help a bit
An' lighten up my load?

SUNDAY DINNER

The folks all went to meetin'
Then come back home to eat,
An' you should hear the jawin'
An' scufflin' 'round of feet!
The wimmin in the kitchen
Rattlin' pan an' pot,
An' all the men are gabbin'
Down aroun' the lot.

The screen door keeps a-slammin'
As the kids run in an' out,
An' so it ain't no wonder
There's some buzzin' flies about.
Grandma sits a-rockin'
In that ancient, squeaky chair.
Aunt Emmy's on the back porch
Plaitin' Jenny's hair.

The young folks all is gigglin'
An' actin' like young fillies.
Their carryin' on is quite enough
To give a man the willies!
Some perches on the banister,
An' some sits in the swing,
But every soul is anxious
For the dinner bell to ring!

I peeped into the dinin' room
An' on the table saw
A heap of fancy vittles
To make you fight yo' paw.
Golden brown fried chicken,
Slabs of country ham,
Bowls of steamin' gravy
An' every kind of jam!

Corn an' squash an' pole beans,
An' milk an' butter too,
An' somethin' in a yeller bowl
That looked like brunswick stew.
An' over on the sideboard
Is rows of cakes an' pies —
I swear that there's enough of 'em
To make you rub your eyes.

The men come in an' take a seat,
An' Preacher asks the blessin',
Though I don't hear jus' what he says
'Cause I can smell that dressin'.
An' then the men folks start to eat.
Gosh! What a noisy lot!
Some is chewin' an' some is blowin'
'Cause all this stuff's still hot!

All the kids has done been shooed
Out in the big back yard,
An' I tell you, sir, it don't seem right
To make their lot so hard.
While the men stuff nigh to bust,
The youngsters have to wait,
An' take their turn a-peepin' in
Or swingin' on the gate.

When the men has et enough
To nearly bust their pants,
Then is when the wimmin
An' the kids can have their chance.
Well, it's sure a real fine dinner,
But it makes me feel right mean
To see them little chillun
A-peepin' through the screen.

FISHIN'

I said, "I'm goin' fishin'
Down by that lazy stream,"
But I never do much fishin'.
I mostly sit an' dream,
An' bask in golden sunlight
That filters through the trees
An' makes a dancin' pattern
On the grass an' dead, brown leaves.

I know there's better fishin'
In that pool aroun' the bend,
But the bank down there is muddy
An' the foliage very thin.
I may not get a nibble
In this cool, secluded spot,
But look at all the shade up here,
The mossy couch I've got!

No wonder I don't catch a fish
Though I've a line an' pole,
For I didn't bring a bit of bait
Down to the fishin' hole.
Oh, well, I'd rather lie aroun'
An' hear the blue jays screamin'.
I guess I should have told the truth
An' said, "I'm goin' dreamin'."

I AIN'T LAZY

Some folks is full of energy
An' start at break of day
A-buildin' things or sellin' stuff,
Or maybe pitchin' hay.

I would like to work some, too,
But I cain't take the strain
Of workin' in an office —
It wearifies my brain.

A shovel handle hurts my hands,
An' I cain't build brick walls
'Cause I cain't stand no dizzy heights.
I'm scared of takin' falls.

I'd like to get some wrenches
An' work on cars an' such,
But I ain't had experience,
An' I don't know too much.

If I could find a real good job
That was lots of fun to do,
I'd work as hard as anyone —
An' be successful too!

But I cain't toss my time away
On dull or messy work,
'Cause I ain't just a common guy,
A worthless, no-count jerk.

Naw, I ain't gonna sweat myself
From early dawn 'till night,
An' it ain't because I'm lazy.
There just ain't no work I like!

DISINTEGRATION

Ah, me, the brilliance of my youth!
My mighty cerebrations!
There was no wiser man I'm sure
In any land or nation.

At twenty-one I knew it all,
Of that there was no doubt,
From nebular hypothesis
To how to cure the gout.

As years rolled on more things I learned.
Minerva watched o'er me.
But old Fate threw the switch at last,
And scuttle me did he.

Into my peaceful, tranquil life
A lovely damsel came.
Her eyes were blue, her hair soft gold,
Her smile a warming flame.

To this sweet child I would impart
My knowledge of all life;
How problems of the world to solve,
How best avoid all strife.

She challenged every thing I said.
Her arguments were strong.
At last corrosive doubt arose.
My gosh! Could I be wrong?

My confidence began to wane.
Assurance left me too.
I'd stood my ground for many years,
But this was something new.

Alas, I am a broken man.
I'll never be the same.
Will some kind soul please tell me,
Is Printup still my name?

I'M A SQUARE

At the art gallery.
The painting's lines were quite grotesque.
The colors glaring — harsh.
It seemed to be a landscape,
A jumbled, streaky marsh.
I moved in closer to the thing,
Bifocals brought to bear.
"Kippered Herrings" read the plate.
I could but stand and stare.

The next one was an exposé
Of some poor tortured soul.
A woman it appeared to be,
Amid surroundings foul.
Bluely bloodless was the flesh,
Gaunt her awkward arm.
I took one look at fevered eyes
And fled in real alarm.

At the music shop.
A group of fuzz-faced "hep cats,"
With long sideburns and pimples,
Were drooling over luscious girls,
Whose bulging curves and dimples
Were used to draw attention
To the latest "rhythm" craze —
A blaring, rocking, vulgar thing
That all fine feeling flays.

Listening to a strident disc
Recorded "hi-fi" style,
Stood a well-bemused young man
With lost, enraptured smile.
I had no idea what could cause
His peaceful, soul-stirred look.
The volume was turned up so high
The very rafters shook.

At the library.
I sit amazed at how much filth
Can rest within the pages
Of books by several authors
Who are currently the rages!
Their characters are scabrous folk
Whose morals are so rotten
The lowest bawd I ever saw
Would call them misbegotten.

Then there's the very brilliant one
Who hides in wordy mazes
Whatever truth his thought may have,
And baffles me with phrases
Concerning vague and abstract things,
And human motivation —
I say, "My friend, please let me off.
I've ridden past my station."

I've seen the perfect sculpturings
Of Michael Angelo,
And paintings where the true-drawn figures
Seemed to live and glow.

I only need to close my door
To shut out raucous noise
And hear some good old "standards"
By Benny Goodman's boys.

To Tristan and Isolde
I can listen every day.
I like the kind of music
That Faith and Chacksfield play.
Longfellow was a poet,
And Burns and Masefield too,
So I will leave to someone else
The brassy, brash and new.

I'm willing for all other men
To have whate'er they want,
Homes like big show windows,
Art that's garish — gaunt.
Music that of my poor nerves
A jangled wreck would make.
Books that leave the feeling
That the whole world's a mistake.

I've reached the peaceful, tranquil spot
Where it just doesn't make
A little bit of difference
What view of me folks take.
So give me soft, sweet music,
Good books and fresh, clean air,
For I don't mind admitting, sir,
That I am just a square.

ME TOO

Humans are a sorry lot,
I've come to hold this true.
But what must people think of me?
I'm somewhat human too.

SORRY MAN!

Tho I ain't been to church in years,
I aim to go some day.
The trouble is I can't agree
With lots of things they say.

And yet I worry now and then
And say, "I'll go next week."
I plan real strong 'till Sunday comes,
Then past the church I sneak.

I guess I shouldn't say such things,
But preachin' leaves me cold.
I know I'm closer to the Lord
Just watchin' cloud banks roll.

He's in the trees and every breeze
And all the great outdoors,
The sunlight and the moonbeams
And sandy, wave-washed shores.

But childhood trainin' put in me
An everlastin' fear
Of even thinkin' such bold thoughts —
They say the Lord can hear!

I guess I ought to swing around
And try hard to conform,
But somehow I'm not made that way,
So I'll just chance the storm.

The thing that really worries me
Is out of this here world —
Some day this mess will all be through
And I'll reach those Gates of Pearl.

And when Saint Peter checks the book
And sees there all the proof,
He may look down his nose and say,
"Sorry, man. You goofed!"

WE KNOW

Some folks, although they are quite wise,
Don't know what goes on in the skies.
They only see the rain and snow
That falls upon the earth below.
But how it starts to drifting down
Is something they have never found.

Our red skinned brother in the West
Is nature's child, and he is blessed
With knowledge of these mystic things,
And Thunder Bird who never sings,
But when he blinks his sleepy eye
Then lightning flashes rip the sky.

Upon his back there is a lake,
And just a little tilt it takes,
When Thunder Bird is flying high,
To splash some water through the sky,
And then it trickles down as rain,
And sun scorched lands are fresh again.

So when the sky's a leaden grey
And fluffy bits drift down all day,
The great Snow Goose is winging out
And winds his feathers blow about,
And we, the pixilated, know
It's just goose down, this stuff called snow.

MUSH HEAD

She isn't over three feet tall
And not yet three years old,
But you should see those big brown eyes,
That smile worth tons of gold.

Her mother warned me to go slow,
"She's quite afraid of men."
I thought, "Oh, brother, just my luck,
Well, here we go again."

That little tyke sat quietly
While I went through my act.
I made a dozen shots or so,
And then began to pack.

I knelt beside my camera case
To put the things away.
She stood and watched my every move
But not a word would say.

Then with no bit of warning
She stepped across the rug
And slipped her arms around me
And gave my neck a hug!

My backbone turned to jelly,
And I swear I almost cried.
I felt as foolish as could be
And fought those tears to hide.

I'm sometimes tough with other folks,
But I'll not kid myself.
I'm just a big, mush-headed jerk
Around that little elf.

THE KID GREW UP

Time was when Cupid was an elf
Whose garments were quite simple.
His raiment was a ribbon red,
Some curls and several dimples.

His armament was just a bow,
Some arrows and a smile.
Though ever a conniving brat,
He was still a charming child.

But times have changed, the kid grew up
And roared in like a Stuka,
Then levelled off and blasted me
With a shattering bazooka!

ADVENTURER

I've shivered in the Arctic nights
Half frozen by the cold,
And watched the wavering Northern Lights
That shimmered green and gold.
I've trod the trackless, barren waste
Of blazing desert sand,
And hacked my way through jungles
In dank miasmic lands.

I've paced the decks of many ships
Through calm and howling storm.
I've struggled with some brawny brutes,
And known rage, fear, alarm.
I've shouted curses at my team
On wild and rocky trails,
While freighting to the pioneers
Supplies of food and mail.

I've stormed great stony battlements,
And fought with savage beasts.
I've starved at times and known great thirst,
And gorged at lavish feasts.
I've dived for pearls and searched for gold
And roamed through every land.
I've lived with men of wealth and grace,
And wild, nomadic bands.

And oft I've sat on sandy shores
And watched the silver moon
Dance with sheer abandon
Across a dark lagoon.
I've known the rapturous murmur
Of deep, contented sighs,
As I felt the clinging softness
Of luscious lips and eyes.

Ah, me, it's been a wondrous life!
I've lived with eager zest,
And earned the right to settle down
And just relax and rest.
To sit and while away my days
In quiet, restful nooks,
But I never could have done these things
Without my dreams and books!

SURE CURE

Once when a kid I had to use
A pair of good though outgrown shoes;
Though patched and shined and fairly neat,
O, brother! How they hurt my feet!

My father stern would scowl and say,
"You *will* wear them to school today."
I'd force them on and blink back tears —
The pain was bad, but worse the fears.

Those days were often more than rough,
But I was made of rugged stuff.
I did survive, grew tall and strong,
But memory of my youth is long.

So now I have an answer rare
To how to banish woe and care.
A way to drive from any brain
All thought of bad luck, grief or strain.

The mind just one main thought can hold,
Or so by wise ones I've been told.
So when toes throb and blisters sting,
You can't think of another thing!

So buy some shoes two sizes small
And stomp all day through street and hall.
By night except for pedal pains
You'll be your normal self again!

BALONEY!

Some Frenchman said, long years ago,
Each man should take a wife.
If things go well then he will lead
A quite contented life.
If things go badly he'll become
No doubt quite philosophic.
I tried to follow his advice,
But now I'm misanthropic.

MY FRIEND

My friend is always ready,
And waiting for my call.
My friend makes no extreme demands,
And quarrels not at all.
My friend can raise me from despair
And fill my head with knowledge.
My friend does not deplore the fact
I never went to college.
My friend has one shortcoming
The poor thing cannot cook.
But that will make no difference,
For you see — my friend's a book.

DEFINITION

Noah Webster, while kissing a maid,
Was discovered by his spouse —
"Why Noah! I'm surprised!" she cried,
And glared as at a louse.

"Ah, no, my dear," said Noah.
"You're astounded — maybe shocked,
While it is I who am surprised,
And I thought that door was locked."

WHY COMPARE?

I'd be silly if I said,
"You're lovely as the moon."
It seems so cold and distant,
And will be gone quite soon.

I'd be silly if I said,
"You're lovely as a rose."
It's just here for the balmy days,
When winter comes, it goes.

I'd be silly if I said,
"You're lovely as the dawn."
Sometimes in the early hours
The rain comes pelting down.

Why compare you with such things?
For when the talk's all through,
The simple fact remaining is —
I'm silly over you!

RODEO

I looked with apprehension
At that quiverin', twitchin' beast
Still penned up tightly in the chute
Awaitin' his release.
His ears were laid back on his skull,
His eyes were flashin' fire,
While some fool cowpoke punched at him
An' added to his ire.

I eased down off the upper rail
An' clutched the buckin' rig.
Never had I seen a horse
That looked so mean an' big!
Then I hollered, "Let 'er buck!"
They flung the gate out wide
An', brother, I'm a-tellin' you,
I took an awful ride.

That brute shot out into the lot
As though by jets propelled,
Then bowed his back an' shot straight up
A-snortin' like all hell!
He came down with a crashin' jolt,
All four legs stiff as posts!
He damn near split me half in two,
An' I knew that I was lost.

I didn't have no time to think
But an idea did flash by —
"I've got an easy chair at home,
Why sit I here? Why? WHY?"
He wound up tight and shot ahead.
The snap nigh broke my neck.
In just five seconds by the clock
He'd made of me a wreck.

It seemed to me I'd been up there
A half an hour or more
A-ridin' that damn hurricane,
An' my head began to roar.
Then with a last great twistin' leap
He threw me into space.
I spun around like a whirlin' top,
An' landed on my face.

That still enraged and savage beast
Came tearin' straight at me,
An' I knew in just two seconds
A bloody pulp I'd be.
I gave a yell and sprang straight up,
Then fell back on the bed —
That was a nightmare I had rode,
Or, brother, I'd be dead!

HANGOVER

A blinding flash, a savage shriek,
A writhing, twisting comet
Tears its way through my poor head.
There's no way to hide from it.

Some demon tightened up the screws
That press into my forehead,
And now he bangs upon my skull,
Creating noises horrid.

My innards feel like jungle snakes,
All coiled and fiercely squirming.
I've wondered how it feels to die,
And now I know I'm learning.

The world is whirling round and round.
About me vultures hover.
I must have had a ball last night,
But Lord! Am I hung over!

WHOOSH

A bee is such a little thing,
But powerful is his wee sting.
It's true no athlete great am I,
But one made me jump ten feet high!

TARGET FOR TODAY

I love my little feathered friends
Who flit about the lawn.
There's mocking bird and Jenny Wren,
And sparrows chirp at dawn.

The cardinals in scarlet robes,
And blue jay's raiment gay,
Lend bits of welcome color
To any gloomy day.

But I am bald, and hatless go
As 'round the yard I'm walking —
I wish they would more careful be
When refuse they are parking!

LINES

There are lots of lines of many kinds,
Some good, some bad, some neither —
Fish lines, chow lines, bent lines,
But some give me a fever.

They are the lines that cascade down
From a blond head to the floor,
And when they curve and sway and swerve
At the right place — these I adore!

But time marches on and all things change.
It's sad, boy, but quite true,
And if you are as old as I,
It's fish lines for me and you!

UNLUCKY DAY

So you're a most unhappy man,
And everything's gone wrong.
You curse your fate and tear your hair
And shout in language strong.

The future seems to be quite dark
With some impending blow.
You're worried, scared, and so afraid
Your fear-drawn face to show!

Now don't you know that each extreme
Makes lesser things seem small?
And so this thing that you fear now
Is not so bad at all.

So don't sit there disconsolate,
Despondent and forlorn —
You had your worst mishap my friend
The day that you were born.

PANACEA

I have my pills
For all my ills
In bottles green or clear,
For aching toes
Or sniffly nose
Or ringings in my ear.

I swallow some
And sit quite glum
And mop my fevered brow,
But I grow worse
As aches I nurse
And think, "I'm sicker now."

Then comes an urge
My woes to purge,
Though pills won't get it done.
I get my rule
And nails and tools,
Then start to have some fun.

I saw and nail
And bang and flail
And have myself a ball.
I plan and draw
And plane and saw
'Till I've no cares at all.

My neighbors' ears
Have rung for years
With all the din I make.
They cuss and swear
But I don't care,
For no more pills I'll take!

MY HOUSE

The giant oaks soar toward the sky
And spread a great green canopy
That casts a cooling shade where I
Can rest and seek repose.
Gleeful bits of sun slip through
And dance about on old soft bricks
And dapple lawn and drink the dew
From waving grass and velvet rose
      On the lawn
      At my house.

The pines, which in some later year
May moan and toss in stormy gale,
Are young, and only whisper clear
Their secrets — wistful, haunting tales.
And blossoms needing sunny rays
To bring their glory to the world,
Grow weary struggling in the shade
And keep their lovely petals furled
      In the borders
      Near my house.

But in a bright spot near the door
Gardenias flanked by waxen leaves
Nod and let their fragrance blow —
The perfume of each vagrant breeze.
At dusk the wood thrush trills his song
In the stately old elm tree
To say farewell to the day that's gone
And bring sweet dreams to me
      As evening comes
      To my house.

Within the warm brown, panelled walls
Are things from far and near,
And many a volume softly calls
To me to roam through pages sere,
Telling tales of great, bold deeds
Or some old dream laid bare.
I read or browse to fill my needs
And seek surcease from care
      In the quiet rooms
      Of my house.

A red-skinned potter made this bowl,
A monk that ancient psalter graved.
This Chinese chest I keep to hold
My rugs and treasured things I've saved.
To India bright bowls of brass
Still lure my restless mind
To dream of ancient, mystic things
And then return in time
      To the hearth
      Of my house.

Souvenirs — things of steel
Brought from fields of strife,
Silver, turquoise, clay and wood
I've gathered 'round to bring to life
Memories of far places strange.
A copper vase o'erlaid with lead
From noisy, dusty, old Baghdad,
Reminds me of someone long dead.
      It was her gift
      For my house.

There's music for my every mood
From lullabys to jazz,
And arias to stir my blood
Or soothe me when I'm sad.
Though ivy-covered walls should hold
Contentment, cheer and peace,
The patient trees and I grow old,
And it's a gloomy, lonesome place,
     This quiet spot
     That's my house.

RECOLLECTIONS

I scarce remember the choking fear
That pressed me shaking to the ground,
Whenever shells exploding near
Filled the air with awful sound.

The jagged shrapnel hissing past
Chilled my soul, and yet
The horror of those fearful nights
I somehow soon forgot.

But oft I think of sunlit vales
And soft, grey-green, new leaves
That rustled in the springtime
On budding olive trees.

The quiet, dreamy, ancient towns,
The Italian countryside,
Remain fresh in my memory
Though the fears of war have died.

KINDRED SPIRITS

I long to hear a wild wind roar,
For erstwhile earthbound spirits soar
When blackened clouds like steeds streak by.
Their flashing eyes rip the somber sky,
And I hear the muffled, rolling boom
Of chariot wheels in the darkening gloom.

I like the windswept stinging spray
That's snatched from waves of leaden grey,
As the ocean's waters writhe and surge,
As though some spirit fierce to purge
In a vast and undulating roll
Like the seething of a tortured soul.

On moonlight nights I've scaled a peak
And watched the shooting stars that streaked
Across a crisp and crystal sky,
As the cool enchanted hours slipped by,
While the wind sang a constant, crooning tune
And the thrill of the night was gone too soon.

We are kindred spirits, the wind and I,
Although I must always sit and sigh
And wish that I could take its place
To whirl myself through boundless space
Like some unfettered, restless god,
And not just sit like a moulding clod!

A WISE MAN

Don't call him "wishy-washy"
'Cause what he says today
Won't sound like what he said last week,
Is not the same some way.

He's not a bit unstable.
He knows what he believes,
But keeps on sifting out the facts
Like gravel through a sieve.

He wants the big, sound, solid truth.
The little stuff can go.
He'll roll a subject back and forth
Until the facts all show.

He's stubborn, that I will admit,
And quite hard to convince,
But he will change if he is shown
A different view makes sense.

And so he sometimes shifts around,
When wrong, tries another slant,
For it's the wise who can change their minds.
The fools are the ones who can't.

WATCH IT!

Making your own self look smart
At another man's expense
May sometimes seem quite clever,
But it doesn't make much sense.

An Oriental custom
That we could emulate,
Is always let each one save face,
And none humiliate.

Sometimes it isn't very hard
To win a round, but then,
It may just be one day you'll find
You've lost a real good friend.

You may be "frank" and critical
And think that's being smart,
But I have news for you, my friend,
You're losing from the start!

Independent you may be,
For friendship give no sou,
But I guarantee you one thing —
You'll be mighty lonesome too.

NOCTURNE

I sank to earth at the forest's edge,
And the coolness under the trees
Was an inky cavern of blackness
Walled in by close-grown leaves.
Spongy moss made a cushion
At the base of a giant oak.
Creatures of night and the darkness
With small sounds the stillness broke.

The silent, friendly moon slipped up
And poured upon the world
A ghostly, silver cascade
That down the hillside swirled,
And made the fields a fairyland
Of shadows mauve and grey,
Cast by waving grasses
That in the moonlight swayed.

The rising wind was fresh and cool
And whirling through the night
Dislodged from dry, reluctant stems
The autumn leaves, and started flights
In long and spinning earthbound glides,
Where, mingling with the mould,
They'll soon replace the tattered rug
Of leaves once red and gold.

How can I tell with clumsy words
The things that filled my soul?
The quiet, poignant loneliness,
And faded hopes untold,
The overwhelming ecstacy
Born of moonlight's magic glow,
That made into a dream world
This bitter place I know.

Some fairy touched me with a wand
And a wondrous gift was mine.
My cares and griefs were banished
And I lost all sense of time.
Deep in reverie and dreams
I mused throughout the night,
And with profound reluctance
Arose with dawn's first light.

My troubles I must lift again,
The weary, heavy load,
And stumble through this lifetime
Down the endless, rocky road.
But the way will be less painful,
My soul more free and light,
If I can only dream sometimes
Through lovely moonlit nights.

SAVE IT

The good advice I freely give
Is neither asked or wanted,
So why should I annoyed be
When my beliefs are flaunted?

I hope from now on I shall be
As quiet as an elf,
And keep my "wisdom" here at home —
I need it all myself!

GRATEFUL

When days are rough
And nights are blue
And I have naught
But trouble,
I'm ever grateful
To the Lord
That I was not
Born double!

YARDSTICK

He who thinks of all men ill
Must surely know himself quite well.

PINE TREE

My love of pine trees goes way back
To carefree boyhood days,
When I scarcely saw their beauty
Though I used them many ways.
I've climbed the slim pine saplings
And swung out into space
As I clung to topmost branches
And rode to earth — quite safe.

I built a pine log cabin
In the deepest forest gloom,
Where the sunlight never ventured,
And no woodland flowers bloomed.
I started all my campfires
With splinters of pitch pine
Chopped from "lightard" stumps,
The quickest-burning kind.

I know the soaring majesty
Of towering feathered kings
Within whose dark green branches
The mountain breezes sing.
I've slipped away from humdrum life
To spend enchanted nights
On carpets of pine needles
That clothe the rocky heights.

I've munched the tasty pinon nut,
So sweet and rich and good.
It's gathered by the Navajos
And highly prized as food.
I've seen the ponderosa pine,
The largest of them all,
And the tiny cone it brings forth —
No other is so small.

Ah! Long I've loved the pine tree
And its sad and wistful song
As it sighs in gentle breezes
Or moans when winds are strong.
And when it comes my time to go,
It will suit my shade just fine,
If you'll wrap my worn out body
In a box of fragrant pine.

LUCKY YOU

I don't know why I love you,
Nor do I ever care!
I only know without you
My life is all too bare.

You say that it's a real good world,
But you've yourself, you see.
And that is all I'd ever want,
But I have naught but me!

DEMON IN MY CLOCK

It seems you just walked through the door,
But clock says it's an hour or more
Since I heard gentle tapping sounds
That caused me from my chair to bound,
To greet you and to hold you near —
The sum of all that I hold dear.

How could time ever fly so fast?
We only sat and talked and laughed,
And I was quite content to be
Just sitting near so I could see
Those merry, dancing, teasing eyes —
And hear contented, gentle sighs.

Ah! me, I guess it's just my luck
To have a demon in my clock
Who whirls at frantic speed each gear
Whenever I can have you near,
And forces them to snail's pace slow
The very moment that you go!

IT'S JUST A THOUGHT

It's just a thought, and not my own,
But please consider this;
The Lord gave us a wondrous world,
But something's gone amiss.

The seas and hills are much the same.
The mountains still are grand.
It seems to me the biggest change
Is with this thing called man.

In Africa God put the blacks.
In Europe men were white.
The Far East was the yellow realm.
Red men held this site.

Could be the trouble started
When we tinkered with the plan.
Caucasian greed for gold and fame
Has tainted every land.

Like children with a torn up clock
We don't know what to do.
The wheels and springs and screws are there,
But the smooth tick-tock is through.

HERITAGE

I never saw my Grandpa
And it always makes me sad
To think that I missed knowing
Such a wonderful Granddad.
I only have a picture
Of a kind and gentle face,
With large, dark eyes and broad, fine brow
And a look of quiet grace.

My mother told me stories
Of his care for those in need,
And how he left his own affairs
All pleas of help to heed,
And how his only treasures
Were those he stored above,
Where I hope they kept a record
Of his many gifts of love.

Grandpa was a peaceful man
But a soldier he was too,
And served with gallant courage
Beneath that cross of blue
On the blood red flag with pure white stars
As he fought with General Lee,
In defense of his conviction
And to keep the Southland free.

With straining back and blackened face
He used his brawny might
To serve his roaring cannon
As he battled for the right.
At Appomattox Court House
With that battered, grey-clad host,
Teardrops streaked his bearded face —
The awful fight was lost.

And so I look with pride and awe
At the pattern laid for me.
How can I ever match his deeds
And worthy of him be?
And the thought fair overwhelms me
That I must be the one
To set the same examples
For a lad — for my grandson.

I WISH

I wish that I could always stand
With shield and flaming sword
Where I could drive away from you
Each ache — each unkind word,
To always guard you from all strife
And ward off every blow,
But if I should do all these things,
Then you'd no stronger grow!
For each must drink his bitter cup,
Must know his share of pain,
And many times be struck to earth,
As many rise again.

I wish that I could even say
Some word to give you strength.
If things could be this way, my dear,
I'd go to any length
To make your whole life happy
And filled with rosy light;
But since I cannot take your place
Then you must stand and fight.
It's always nicest if you win,
But if you've lost or won,
The only thing that really counts
Is how the race was run.

NOW I SEE

There were some lovely flowers by the trail
I failed to see, when rushing on my way,
For ever fast and faster was I driven,
And grew more weary with each passing day.

But now I'm drawing closer to the end,
And weak and heavy-limbed I stumble on.
My many burdens bow me to the ground.
The race will soon be lost — or won.

But even as I falter and grow faint,
I see that there are beauties to behold
In many simple blossoms by the way
That I crushed in swifter days of old.

RESIGNATION

Tonight the air was so, so still,
I heard leaves brush the window sill.
Like wounded birds they spiralled down
To carpet all the bare, cool ground.

And then an errant, chilly breeze
Twisted limbs of old oak trees,
And jostled from each checkered cup
The warm brown, polished acorn crop.

They drummed staccato on the roof
And gave of winter's coming proof.
Leafless branches made dark lace
Across the full moon's silver face.

The beauty of these autumn days
Is warming as the sun's soft rays,
But nameless fear gnaws at my soul,
Distilled from many aches of old.

With coming of another spring
Bright leaves will clothe the trees again,
Though little will it bring to me.
Still hopeless, dreamless shall I be.

TOPPY'S GONE

There's something wrong with this old place.
 It's gloomy as a tomb.
That's why I sit and stare at space
 Or pace about the room.
It can't be that the house has changed,
 The trees — the big front lawn;
I think I know what it must be —
 It's just that Toppy's gone.

There is no sand upon the floor,
 No rocks piled in the chair.
"Number nine" is not "lined up" —
 There's a stillness in the air.
The "big gawage" is empty now,
 And as sure as you are born,
This house will be a lonesome place,
 Now that Toppy's gone.

"Moochie" pads from door to door,
 And then he looks at me
And seems as though he wants to ask,
 "What happened to those three?"
His top-knot has smoothed back in place
 But still he looks forlorn,
For I guess by now he's figured out
 That little Toppy's gone.

No flowers lose their lovely heads,
 For no "Baby helps Dan-Dan."
Even the "pikes" are right in place
 And lined up in the stand.
The choo-choo rumbles on its way
 With " 'boose" and noisy horn,
And I wish they'd run it somewhere else
 Now that T-Toppy's gone.

I go out to the "salt mine"
 And at my desk I sit,
And think, "I need my glasses changed,
 My vision blurs a bit."
I try to do the things I should
 And work 'till nearly dawn —
But I can't work this mood away
 For I know Toppy's gone.

LAMENT

I love to watch your fingers
As they dance across the keys,
Extracting pompous tonal things,
Or airy melodies.

Your impish grin and bouncy gait
Are something to behold!
I wish I could ignore the truth —
I'm swiftly growing old.

'Twould be a very gladsome thing
If I could keep you near
To brighten up this gloomy place
With songs I like to hear.

But I must face the dreary fact,
The rotten trick of fate.
Either I was born too soon,
Or you were born too late!

MY PRAYER

Lord, I've got a problem
    And it puzzles me a lot.
It's just that I appear to be
    A heathen when I'm not.
Of course it isn't what folks think
    That causes me concern,
But it's just that there is such an
    Awful lot for me to learn!

I've listened to some brainy men
    And tried to find the truth.
I've searched through many different books
    Just looking for some proof.
But each one says a different thing —
    They seldom can agree.
So how on earth am I to know
    Which road was meant for me?

There are so many different brands
    Of worship in the world,
Competing with each other
    For each errant, truant soul.
They all are so dogmatic
    And say, "We have the key!"
Their rituals may suit them, Lord,
    But they're just not for me.

I see them build their temples,
    Great piles of brick and steel,
And they say, "This is the Lord's house,

And you must come here and kneel."
Now if it makes them better
    To go there once a week,
Then I've no quarrel with their plan,
    But my own way I seek.

I seem to see tired, sandalled feet
    Along a dusty trail
That winds through ancient olive groves
    And toward a distant sail
Where men have gathered on the shore
    To hear the story told
Of all the world's salvation,
    Of the pathway to the fold.

It's such a quiet picture.
    No glitter, pomp or show,
And it contrasts very strangely
    With the churches that I know.
So won't it be all right, Lord,
    If I just stay outdoors
And seek you in the heavens
    And among the twinkling stars?

To some men you are Allah.
    Some use a different name.
Great Spirit, God, Jehovah —
    I think they mean the same.
The great "World Soul" of Hindu faith,
    The Lord, and Yaweh too,
Are just the names that other men
    Have used — and all mean you.

I know you're in those piles of brick.
     Of course! You're everywhere.
But by the self-same token,
     You're out here in the air.
And I can sit on mossy ground,
     Or on a log or stone,
And look up at the azure sky —
     That's my cathedral's dome.

The forests are the pillars
     And a shady lane the aisle.
I have a real fine feathered choir
     That sings in grandest style.
If I should need an altar,
     What's better than that stone
That you yourself placed in this spot
     Where I can think — alone?

I'll try to live a good life, Lord,
     Work by the "Golden Rule,"
But please be patient with my faults.
     Sometimes I'm such a fool!
I'll be grateful for the good
     That comes my way, and then,
I'll try to take my punishments
     With strength and grace — Amen.

BON VOYAGE

You want to go your own fine way
And make your own mistakes.
With high excitement run the race
And hope for dazzling breaks.

You're much like me, my little friend.
I once was headstrong too,
And I was deaf to much advice
That now I know was true.

So may the Fates be good to you.
Go — laugh and dance your fill.
And may they be most kind to you
When making out the bill!

ARIZONA PAGEANT

I wandered from the hogan
Into the chilly night.
The world was wrapped in inky robes.
The stars were jewels bright.
A wild wind whistled from the hills
And wrapped itself about me.
I sniffed the fragrance of the sage,
And felt ecstatic — free.

Then high above the somber hills
The sky grew slowly bright,
And little cloud banks here and there
Were touched with rosy light.
Soon from behind a jagged ridge
There peeped a shining head,
And ghostly mists and shadows
Became alarmed and fled.

Across the heavens sailed the sun
Against a cobalt sky,
Revealing many varied scenes
That in these regions lie;
The mountains and the deserts
And the brilliant cactus blooms,
The flocks that graze the valleys,
And the weavers at their looms.

Higher, hotter, climbed the sun;
It seemed a blazing torch
That tried to sear the universe,
The very earth to scorch.
All living things slowed to a walk.
On sand the heat waves danced.
Lizards scurried shade to shade;
The sizzling passage chanced.

The brassy orb slid down the sky
And neared the mesa land
Where there a natural stage was set
For plays both wild and grand.
The Sun God in his gleaming robes
Approached the altar high,
A huge flat rock of red sandstone
Flung upward toward the sky.

Then as he settled on his throne
A pagan host disclosed,
Arrayed in gorgeous splendor
In cloaks of flashing rose,
That quickly changed to purple
And shades of blue-grey hue.
He lingered there a moment,
Then golden darts he threw.

Heavenly dancers moved about
With slow and stately grace,
And changed into a fairyland
The desert's sand and waste,
As every color, shade and hue
Across the land they rolled,
And every jutting rock and crag
They splashed with molten gold.

The flaming symphony was done.
The Sun God slipped from view.
The colors slowly faded
As night the curtains drew.
A cool breeze rustled through the sage.
A coyote howled a dirge.
Dusk spread its soft gray mantle.
Rough shapes slowly merged.

A weird song blended with the breeze,
A high-pitched, haunting thing.
A Navajo rode toward his home.
How good that he should sing!
A fitting encore for this show,
The grandest ever seen.
I drew a deep, belated breath,
And slipped away to dreams.